PASSWORD
SECRETS

MORE BOOKS COMING SOON
BY LORENZO ZESATI

MEETING SECRETS
HOW TO GENERATE NEW IDEAS

All current and future books are available at

www.TekkieTeks.com/Products

PASSWORD SECRETS

CONCEALING YOUR IDENTITY

TO PROTECT YOUR ACCOUNTS, EMAILS,
COMPUTERS, AND DOCUMENTS

LORENZO ZESATI

THINKBODY
PUBLISHING

This book is a gift to

Given by

Because we care about you concealing your identity

Published in the United States by ThinkBody Publishing

This publication is designed to provide general information regarding the subject matter covered. However, laws and practices often vary from state to state and are subject to change. Because each factual situation is different, specific advice should be tailored to the particular circumstances. For this reason, the reader is advised to consult with his or her own IT Support Specialist regarding their specific situation.

The author has taken reasonable precautions in the preparation of this book and believe the facts presented in this book are accurate as of the date it was written. However, the author assumes no responsibility for any errors or omissions. The author specifically disclaims any liability from the use or application of the information contained in this book, and the information is not intended to serve as legal,

Hardcover ISBN: 978-0-9963693-0-5

1st Edition, May 2021

Printed in the United States of America.

DEDICATIONS

This book is dedicated to my wife Michelle and my three Mastermind friends Jason Gonzales, Mario Ascoli, and Ray Madaghiele

MICHELLE ZESATI

My amazing wife, the love of my life, and the person who taught me how to understand love and further my growth with God. Since 1999, she has been with me through it all, the start and growth of TekkieTeks and the difficulties of life we have faced together. She has patiently been waiting for me to publish my first book. She continues to be the super special person God has blessed me with. Together we have three amazing children who are special in their own way. Love you guys and I always thank God for being blessed with such an amazing family.

I love you Michelle and Thank you from the bottom of my heart.

JASON GONZALES

Jason is one of the youngest and smartest business professionals I know who has become an amazing friend. Since the day we met, he has been patiently teaching me so much about the alternative ways of doing business online. We continue to meet three days of the week to growing TekkieTeks, publishing my books, and converting my knowledge into online courses. He continues to help me transition from my old ways of business thinking to using social media, marketing tools, and the various platforms to have TekkieTeks succeed online. All I can say is that Jason has been such an astonishing friend. I will always thank God for putting him in my path, especially in the current stage of my personal and professional life.

Thank you Jason.

MARIO ASCOLI

Mario, who I met at Apple, has been that one friend who continues to believe in and support me through it all. He is like that one baseball coach who believes you can get a home run one day even though you keep striking out. Mario has been there so many times to just listen to my crazy business ideas and even though I have changed my mind so many times, he continues to encourage me to hit that home run. Mario has been and continues to be a genuine friend who cares about my success and well-being. He is like an angel sent from God to make sure that I stay on course with God's plan and to guide me and my business in the right direction of loving and serving others.

Thank you Mario.

RAY AND LYN MADAGHIELE

Ray and his wife Lyn, where do I start, they are by far one of the most amazing and vibrant couples I have ever met. They have become what I consider my business parents and personal/professional coaches in all areas of my life. They have affected me the most on the business and spiritual side of things. Ray and I continue to meet every Friday to help each other with our new online business ventures. We share and bounce new ideas with each other. We compare and implement what we have learned about the alternative ways and tools of doing business online. Ray has been very instrumental in guiding me through the book process and sharing his experiences as an author and entrepreneur. He has helped me launch my new books, notebooks, products, and services. I always look forward to our Friday meetings because of the excitement of learning something new and hearing his personal stories as well.

Thank you Ray and Lyn.

THANK YOU

I, Lorenzo Zesati, want to THANK YOU so much for purchasing your very own "Password Secrets" book. I hope you enjoy it, and we welcome any future referrals. Please also consider buying the "Password Secrets Notebook" which complements this book.

With everything going online, it has become somewhat of a stressful ordeal trying to keep up with so many accounts and different password requirements. Especially when most accounts now are requiring you to have a strong password. For the past 21 years, we have been working with clients in securing their accounts and creating strong passwords. We felt we needed to package all those years of experience into this book in order to help more people who are not our clients understand how to create strong passwords and secure their accounts as well.

NEED YOUR HELP

We value and always welcome your feedback, ideas, and improvements to continue to make this "Password Secrets" book better each year for more people to enjoy. Please email us at **WeCare@TekkieTeks.com** with the subject line "PWS Improve" for any of your feedback, ideas, and improvements. Thank You from all of us at TekkieTeks.

Sincerely,

Lorenzo Zesati

CONTENTS

CHAPTER 1
PASSWORDS **Page 1**

- KEEP IT ORGANIZED
- ACCOUNTS AND PASSWORDS
- OUR HOPE
- THE "NEVERS"
- COMMONLY USED PASSWORDS
- WEAK PASSWORDS AND BEING HACKED
- HOW OFTEN SHOULD I CHANGE MY PASSWORDS?
- NAMING YOUR PASSWORDS
- PASSWORD CHARACTERS

CHAPTER 2
OUR STRATEGIES **Page 19**

- 5-FINGER PASSWORD STRATEGY SYSTEM
- PASSPHRASES
- AUTHENTICATION
- PARTIAL PASSWORDS
- DISGUISING YOUR PASSWORDS
- NAKED PASSWORDS
- PASSWORD SECRETS NOTEBOOK SAMPLES

CHAPTER 3
EMAIL ADDRESSES & SETTINGS

Page 47

- DIFFERENT EMAILS ADDRESSES
- EMAIL ALIAS
- EMAIL ADDRESSES
- IMPORTANT BUSINESS EMAIL ADDRESSES
- NONCRITICAL BUSINESS EMAIL ADDRESSES
- ALIAS BUSINESS EMAIL ADDRESSES
- IMPORTANT PERSONAL EMAIL ADDRESSES
- FUN PERSONAL EMAIL ADDRESSES
- ALIAS PERSONAL EMAIL ADDRESSES
- ALL EMAIL ADDRESSES
- CLOSING OR DELETING EMAIL ACCOUNTS
- EMAIL SETTINGS
- MICROSOFT EXCHANGE OR GOOGLE G-SUITE
- PASSWORD SECRETS NOTEBOOK SAMPLES

CHAPTER 4
COMPUTERS, SMARTPHONES, & DEVICES **Page 75**

- WINDOWS LOCAL VS EMAIL ACCOUNT
- BIOS PASSWORDS
- MAC COMPUTERS
- GUESS USER ACCOUNTS FOR MACS
- STANDARD USER PROFILE FOR WINDOWS
- PHONES
- ENCRYPTION FOR WINDOWS
- ENCRYPTION FOR MACS
- RECOMMENDATIONS
- PASSWORD SECRETS NOTEBOOK SAMPLES

CHAPTER 5
DOCS, SOFTWARE, APPS, & LICENSES **Page 91**

- DOCUMENTS
- SOFTWARE
- SUBSCRIPTIONS
- RENEWALS (TURN THEM OFF)
- PASSWORD SECRETS NOTEBOOK SAMPLES

CHAPTER 6 **YOUR ISP & WIRELESS NETWORK & IOT DEVICES**	**Page 99**

- INTERNET SERVICE PROVIDER (ISP)
- ROUTER
- WIRELESS NETWORK (WN)
- PASSWORD SECRETS NOTEBOOK SAMPLES

CHAPTER 7 **OTHER PEOPLE & YOUR CC HISTORY**	**Page 111**

- OTHER PEOPLE'S PASSWORD
- OTHER PEOPLE WHO YOU SHARED PASSWORDS WITH
- YOUR KID'S PASSWORDS
- HIRING FREELANCERS AND PROFESSIONALS
- YOUR CREDIT CARD HISTORY
- PASSWORD SECRETS NOTEBOOK SAMPLES

CHAPTER 8 **RESOURCES**	**Page 125**

- PASSWORD SECRETS NOTEBOOK PURCHASE
- OUR MEMBERSHIP BENEFITS
- EXTRAS, DISCOUNTS, & SUPPORT AS NEEDED
- THREE MEMBERSHIP PLANS
- FREE TEKKIE TUESDAYS WEBINAR
- URGENT IT SUPPORT

CHAPTER

1

PASSWORDS

KEEP IT ORGANIZED

As you begin to read this book and understand the password secrets, please consider using and documenting your passwords in the "Password Secrets Notebook." If you have not yet purchased your very own Password Secrets Notebook, please visit **www.TekkieTeks.com/Products**.

It is very important to make sure you keep the notebook clean, neat, and organized as much as possible. Please avoid using it for scrabbling, writing quick notes here and there, or to record someone's phone number. Please take the notebook seriously and strictly use it to organize and ONLY STORE information that relates to your:

- Own passwords
- Email Addresses and Accounts
- Computers, Smartphones, and Devices
- Documents, Software, Apps, and Licenses
- ISP, Wireless Network, and IoT devices
- Other People's Passwords
- Credit Card History

ACCOUNTS AND PASSWORDS

Now-a-days, you are required to have different, but strong passwords, for your accounts, computers, smartphones, and many other devices that require some sort of credentials to log into. Some vendors require that you make your passwords very strong while others require a less secure password that have a minimum of eight or less characters.

With so many accounts and passwords to worry about, it has become very frustrating for many people, and we have seen it first-hand with our clients. Eventually, what ends up happening is that most people just give up and do not want to deal with the confusion, disorganization, and headache as to what passwords go to what accounts and where to store them. So, they use the same username and weak or simple passwords for all their accounts.

In fact, since 1999 we have seen too many of our clients become frustrated and stressed out trying to manage their accounts and passwords. It has become even more stressful trying to come up with new passwords each time they need to change their passwords.

What we have noticed is that the frustration and stress come from:

- Having too many passwords to organize.
- Forgetting their new password and having to reset it again.
- Having to find their password.
- Not having one place to store their passwords.
- Not being able to use the previous same password.
- Not being able to change the previous password slightly.
- Sharing the passwords with strangers or people.
- Trying to come up with a different and stronger password than the one before.
- Trying to remember the longer or new password.
- Working together with a spouse or partners to come up with an agreeable password.

OUR HOPE

It is our hope that through the "Password Secrets" we can help remove some of the frustration and stress that comes when creating or dealing with passwords. Password Secrets is packed with information to help you understand passwords that will conceal your identity and protect your accounts, email addresses, computers, smartphones, docs, and other people who share their passwords with you. We have also combined the most asked questions by our clients when dealing with passwords. We also hope that you:

- Take the time to understand and organize your accounts and passwords into the password secrets notebook.
- Keep track of all your accounts and passwords in one location.
- Use our strategies to understand how to create strong passwords with ease.
- Help you use patterns and different numbers of character combinations to generate your passwords.
- Make it easy to create different usernames and passwords for your accounts.
- Use "Passphrases" with some of your passwords.
- Make strong passwords easy for you to recall but seem long and complicated to others.
- Learn how to name your strong passwords.

THE "NEVERS"

Before we start to dive into understanding your passwords, let us first focus on the "NEVERS" and what not to do with your passwords.

SHARE IT

Never give or share your passwords to:

- Strangers you just met, especially the tech guys you met at the local tech store or on the phone.
- Friends, because a friend can accidentally pass your passwords along to others or even become an ex-friend and abuse it.
- Kids, because if they know your passwords, they will share it and sometimes show off that they know your password.

ONE PASSWORD

Don't just use one password for all your accounts, especially when all the accounts have the same username and passwords.

From our experience, we have seen too many of our clients use the same username and one password for all their accounts.

The reason for this strategy is that it is just a simple way for them to remember their login information, but it is also extremely easy for their accounts to get hacked. We don't recommend this at all. Please avoid having one password for everything.

HIDING PASSWORD

Never hide your passwords in the following places:

- **Monitor**. The most common place we have seen clients tape their passwords has been on the back, front, or under the monitor. This is just an easy way for them to recall their log-in password to their computer.
- **Computers or Desk**. Under or on the computer (mostly laptops), somewhere on the desk, like under the desk tray or drawer. Please avoid placing any passwords on your computers, smartphones, or devices. Avoid storing your passwords in the Notes app.
- **Keyboard, Mouse, or Mouse Pad**. Avoid hiding your password inside the mouse, underneath the keyboard or mouse pad.

We will introduce how to disguise passwords in Chapter 2 to help when you must physically tape, type, or write it somewhere on your computer, desk, or Notes app.

EASY TO GUESS PASSWORD

Avoid easy to guess or predictable passwords. There have been many times that we have been able to guess our client's passwords by some basic information we knew about them or the hints they provided on their computer's profile. Some used their kids' or wife's name. Some even used their computer's profile name as the password.

Your goal is to avoid simple and predictable passwords to protect you and prevent various types of threats.

SECURITY QUESTIONS

Some online accounts and when setting up a local profile account in Windows, will ask to provide up to three security questions.

When it comes to security questions, we recommend NOT providing the correct answers, instead provide answers that are fake, funny, or just don't make sense to security questions being asked.

USERNAMES

When setting up new accounts, most accounts will ask for an email as your username. To improve your protection and when possible, **please use a custom username**. Just make sure to document the correct spelling of the username in the password secrets notebook. We recommend not using common usernames like your:

- First and Last name
- Last and First name
- First or Last name only
- First initial with Last name
- Last initial with First name

Instead we recommend a unique or custom username.

For example:

- **BigJohnATT**: for the username, you will not use your first name first (John), but instead put 3 to 4 characters in front your name such as "BigJohn" and then add 3 to 4 characters of the company the account is associated with.
- **Baseball95**: it can also be your favorite sport followed by your most successful year in baseball.

You get the idea, create a custom username that works best for you because adding a custom username adds another layer of protection.

SPACES

Avoid using a space or spaces in your passwords. Working with our clients, we ran into many problems identifying or deciphering their passwords. Even though they wrote their password in their notebook, sometimes it created confusion for the clients, us tech people, and others on trying to figure out their password. In the end, we had to reset their passwords.

Some accounts do allow spaces, but it can get a little confusing when storing your password in the password secrets notebook. We highly recommend avoiding **spaces** in passwords.

FULL PASSWORD

Never show your full password within any program and especially your browsers. We will discuss later how to use partial passwords or disguising your passwords.

COMMONLY USED PASSWORDS

In addition, to the "NEVERS" we also recommend avoiding commonly used passwords. We are all guilty of using simple, but common passwords. Most of our client's love using the 123 or 1234 passwords. We have compiled a list of the most common passwords used by some of our clients shown below.

123 or 1234	12345
123456	abc123 or 123123
12345678	1234567890
111111 or other repeated #s	LzLz (initials twice)
Million$	Millions
Iloveyou	Pic1 or picture1
passw0rd	p@ssw0rd
password1	Password
qwerty	asdfghj
zxcvbnm	qwaszx
Using only the numbers from their cell	
Only using their street address numbers	

password (yes, the word password)
Using their spouses or kid's first names
First name backwards with birthday year
First name backwards
Using the first part of email for their email password
Using initials followed by their birthday lz101254 or LZ101254 or LZ101254

WEAK PASSWORDS AND BEING HACKED

In the 21 years of supporting our clients, we have had a few clients call us after they have been hacked because of a weak password they had used, or they gave their password to the person on the phone when our clients called one of those fake Apple, Google, or Microsoft support numbers.

In all honesty, it takes tons of more work to **recover** from a hacked account than to simply create a strong password from the start. We will introduce our "**5-Finger Password Strategy (5FPS)**" System and other strategies in Chapter 2 to help you understand and create strong passwords.

We understand that strong passwords require some work to create and enter every time. But putting that extra little effort UPFRONT will protect you and your accounts in the long run and avoid you going through the process of recovering from a hacked account.

Witnessing firsthand what our clients went through, we strongly recommend avoid using weak passwords and giving someone your passwords who you don't know personally. Be very protective and ask a lot of questions about the person or company you are giving access to any of your business and/or personal accounts, especially any financial accounts that relate to your money.

HOW OFTEN SHOULD I CHANGE MY PASSWORDS?

Many experts will recommend changing your passwords every 90 days. At first, we agreed with them but then working with our clients, most have complained that changing their passwords every 90 days was too frequent. For instance, it makes more sense to change your password based on the following situations:

COMPROMISED

If you feel or think your **password has been compromised**. Change it right away.

Try also using **https://monitor.firefox.com** to see if you have been part of an online data breach. Firefox Monitor allows you to find out if any of your email accounts have been breached. If they have been breached, you can change your password right away and sign up to have all your accounts monitored.

Also, try using Google's **Password Checkup** to check the strength and security of your saved passwords. This will help you find out if your email has been compromised and get advice on what you need to do.

SAME

When you have overused or used the same password on too many of your accounts, when this occurs, we recommend it is time to change the password.

IMPORTANCE

The **Importance** of your account, the more important the account is to you, the more often you might have to change your passwords. We will be going into more details on how often to change your passwords.

SHARED

If you have shared your passwords with too many people then it's time to change it.

REQUIRED

Some accounts require that you change the password every number of months. If they recommend doing it, we recommend you follow their recommendations.

BE PROACTIVE

Of course, if you want to be a little more proactive to prevent and not worry about having your password compromised, please make a normal routine of changing your password every "X" number of days that work best for you, such as every 30, 60, or 90 days.

NAMING YOUR PASSWORDS

One clever way to openly share your password with your spouse or someone who knows your password is for the two of you to agree on a **name or secret code word** for your passwords.

This way when they asked you "What is the password for ...?" like my wife does, instead of spilling out the password in front anyone (like our kids), you can simply provide the name of the password to trigger what password was used. Your goal is to avoid someone knowing your password when you have to share it out loud.

This only works when you and the other person know the assigned name or secret code. Naming your password is optional but give it a try to see if it works for you, because this approach doesn't work for everyone. However, we do recommend documenting the name of the password in the password secrets notebook.

PASSWORD CHARACTERS

One last point before we get into our "**5-Finger Password Strategy (5FPS)**" System, is understanding the type of special characters you can use with your passwords. We recommend that you consider using some of the following characters with your passwords:

- Letters (capital or lower-case)
- Numbers
- Special Characters such as:

&	Ampersand	*	Asterisk
@	At sign	\	Backslash
^	Caret	,	Comma
:	Colon	$	Dollar sign
"	Double quote	=	Equal sign
!	Exclamation	`	Grave accent
>	Greater than	{	Left brace
[	Left bracket	(	Left Parenthesis
<	Less than	-	Minus
#	Number sign	%	Percent

+	Plus	.	Period
?	Question mark	- }	Right brace
]	Right bracket	)	Right Parenthesis
;	Semicolon	'	Single quote
/	Slash	~	Tilde
_	Underscore	|	Vertical bar

You can consider using a:	
$ instead of an S	+ instead of T
$ instead of an S	1 instead of an L
+ instead of T	@ instead of A
You get the ideas	

CHAPTER

2

OUR STRATEGIES

5-FINGER PASSWORD STRATEGY SYSTEM

Back in the early days of passwords, we were told that a simple four to eight-character password was sufficient, but nowadays, the four to eight-character password doesn't apply to all accounts because not all accounts are created equal and will strictly depend on the importance of the account. With that being said, we are so happy to introduce the "**5-Finger Password Strategy (5FPS)**" System.

Strong passwords have always been the first line of defense against unauthorized access to your accounts, and a good deterrent when it comes to protecting any account that requires some form of login credentials, especially your computers.

The strength of a password is very important in protecting your accounts. We feel that the more important your account is to you, the stronger the password you should create for that account.

To understand what we mean and how the 5FPS works

Start by placing your right hand with open fingers in front of you with palm facing left and having your right thumb pointing towards your chest or heart. Each finger will represent the strength and type of password you will be creating.

For example, your "thumb" is the closest to your chest or heart, so you want your "thumb" passwords to be the strongest passwords for all accounts that are **very important** to you. The thumb password will be the most secure password you have in comparison to the other fingers.

To go into further details about the 5FPS, we have provided a table style format for each finger. These tables are laid out to include password examples, strength of each password, when to change them, and who to share them with.

THUMB FINGER PASSWORDS

This is the strongest of all passwords and should be a 20 to 30 character long and strong password. Since the thumb password is the closest finger to your heart, please only share with your spouse.

If you are not married, please give the thumb password to one of your parents, but not your boy/girlfriend. Store your password in the password secrets notebook as soon as you create it and avoid doing it sometime later because most of the times you will forget.

We recommend changing the password every six months, but this is just a recommendation, we leave it up to you as to how often you should change the passwords for your very important accounts.

THUMB FINGER PASSWORDS
PASSWORD EXAMPLES
!Rick#05Joey#11Ruth#21! Rick#05&Joey#11&Ruth#21 EnjoyBiking@Park#2021! 5KidsLovePlaying!88 #16SoftballTeam_2021! @3751JohnB&@5678GinaB
SHARE WITH
Share only with your spouse, parents, or people you truly trust and will not share it with others or come back to use it again you.
WHERE TO USE
Any Bank or financial accounts, Credit Cards, PayPal, Investments, QuickBooks Online, Merchant Accounts, Drive Encryptions, or what you consider *VERY IMPORTANT*.
STRENGTH: 20 to 30 characters
CHANGE: Every 6 months

Using Patterns

When it comes to creating strong passwords for your very important accounts, one recommended strategy is to use repeated groups of patterns in your passwords. Because trying to remember a 20 to 30-character long password is going to be difficult.

Instead, use patterns that can be associated with some areas of your personal or professional life to easily create and remember your passwords. For example, let's say you have three kids with names and college graduate dates of:

- 1) Ricky and April 23, 2001
- 2) Joey and June 17, 2011
- 3) Beth and December 7, 2017

To achieve the strength of 20 to 30 characters. We are going to create a password like:

!Rick#01Joey#11Beth#17!

As you can see we started and ended with the password with a special character of "!" and added the "#" before the numbers to help increase the strength. You can add whatever special characters you like in whatever order makes sense to you. The key here is to notice the pattern, we used the oldest kid first, by using **Rick#01** and then repeated the patten for all the other two kids. The main goal here is to make the thumb passwords long but easy for you to remember them. Another example of using special characters with this password would be adding “&”:

Rick#01&Joey#11&Beth#17

Just replace the “!” with “&” between each name. Be creative and find the patterns that work best for you to make it easy for you to remember the password.

A second might be:

MomSmi>0623&DadSmi>0521

Mom or Dad is the first part of the password, then “Smi” is the first three letter of their last name, then add the “>” and “&” special characters, and finally the numbers associated with some special date or random numbers.

Remember, you don’t have to use your real information as part of passwords, you can make up any name, pattern, and numbers. Just make sure to write down your passwords in the password secrets notebook.

INDEX FINGER PASSWORDS

Now you are getting further away from your heart and landed on the index finger, your passwords should be a little weaker than the thumb passwords but stronger than the middle finger passwords. These passwords we recommend using between 17 to 20 characters. You can continue to use patterns with the index finger passwords, as well.

It is worth mentioning right now, to always share all your passwords with your spouse. With index finger passwords, you can share with kids over the age of 21, family members like your parents, brothers, or sisters.

You can also go as far as sharing with your in-laws (this is optional) and up to you depending on the accounts and your relationship with them. But that is it, no one else should know this password.

Once again, how often to change the passwords, we will always leave it up to you. We just offer our recommendations based on our experiences personally and with our clients.

INDEX FINGER PASSWORDS
PASSWORD EXAMPLES
1983Base2Ball*1989 !MetMyWifeN[1989] (HomeRunSlugger)1989 =3751955%BaseB@!! 5KidsLovePlaying!88
SHARE WITH
Spouse Kids over 21 Your parents, and siblings Maybe your In-Laws
WHERE TO USE
Medical, Memberships, Online Shopping, Apple ID, Emails Accounts, Computers Logins, Dropbox, OneDrive, Google Drive, Amazon Photos, Wi-Fi, Costco, and Insurances.
STRENGTH: 17 to 20 characters
CHANGE: Every 6 to 9 months

MIDDLE FINGER PASSWORDS

Now you landed on the middle finger, these passwords we recommend having between 13 to 16 characters. You can share with your children under the age of 21, relatives, and close friends you have known for five years or more.

We recommend using the middle finger passwords when sharing our Netflix accounts with my siblings or sisters-in-law.

Another example might be where everyone in the family share one computer, where you don't mind using a shared password. You can also share this password with companies and vendors you hire to help you.

MIDDLE FINGER PASSWORDS
PASSWORD EXAMPLES
LoveMyKids2008 Bike_Forever71 BaSe_BALL@1989 @1955Lz@2010Mz
SHARE WITH
Spouse Kids under 21 In-Laws. Cousins and other relative. Very close friends Companies or vendors
WHERE TO USE
Guest Wi-Fi, Router Login, Apps (Chipotle or Click-A-Fil), Software login (Malwarebytes, AVG, Norton), Kid's School or Online Accounts, Games (Minecraft or Nintendo), WordPress, Wix, Spotify, Hulu, and Netflix.
STRENGTH: 13 to 16 characters
CHANGE: Every 12 months

RING FINGER PASSWORDS

Now you landed on the ring finger, these passwords we recommend between 9 to 12 characters.

You can share this password with co-workers, new friends you just met, professional service providers such as your Internet Service Providers (ISP), professionals you hire, and tech guys at the local tech stores. Keep in mind that you still need to guard these passwords to some degree.

When you are required to provide some stranger a password to setup a new account, configure a new phone, or give a tech a temporary password to setup your Wi-Fi, the ring finger passwords are best for quick, simple, and temporary passwords. You will eventually change the password to either a middle or ring finger type of password.

RING FINGER PASSWORDS
PASSWORD EXAMPLES
@Broadway-13 $MoneySmart$ BaSe_BALL@89 #3751955-LnZ
SHARE WITH
Co-workers, Friends you have known for a short time, Clients, Companies, and Vendors
WHERE TO USE
Comcast, Cox, ATT, T-Mobile, Verizon, or Pixabay
STRENGTH: 9 to 12 characters
CHANGE: Every 1 to 2 years

PINKY FINGER PASSWORDS

The pinky finger is the one finger furthest away from your heart. This password is what we consider the "**I don't care if someone steals or knows**" my password. You can share this password with anyone you want.

It is the least important password and it's not a big deal if someone knows it or has access to your accounts associated with these passwords.

PINKY FINGER PASSWORDS
PASSWORD EXAMPLES
#375195lz Lorenzo375 John2021! MyWife2004
SHARE WITH
Share away with anyone
WHERE TO USE
Any account that is not important for you.
STRENGTH: 5 to 8 characters
CHANGE: Every 2 to 5 years

FINAL THOUGHT

Where and how you use the "**5-Finger Password Strategy (5FPS)**" System will be based on your decision to determine how important the accounts are to you and how strong you really need to assign the strength of your passwords. You will have to make the decision and manage what passwords go where and how you use the passwords for each account.

PASSPHRASES

We have been mostly talking about using passwords that contain 5 to 30 characters, but another strategy to consider is the use of passphrasing.

When you use passphrases, it is just a flow of random words or a sentence that only makes sense to you and the person you are sharing it with.

If you find it difficult to come up with strong passwords, consider using passphrases so that you can get to the strength and number of characters we described under each finger in our "**5-Finger Password Strategy (5FPS)**" System.

A passphrase will be much easier to create, remember, and can be relatively long or whatever length you want. For example, using our "**5-Finger Password Strategy (5FPS)**" System you can use passphrases such as:

Thumb Finger	!WeLove2Shop@CostcoAllDay!
	20 to 30 Characters

Index Finger	!WeLove2Shop@Costco!
	17 to 20 Characters

Middle Finger	!WeLove2Shop@!	
	13 to 16 Characters	

Ring Finger	#143Costco!
	9 to 12 Characters

Pinky Finger	Costco7%
	5 to 8 Characters

You get the idea, get creative when using passphrases. We have an amazing client and good friend, Shelby Lozano, who owns King Cobra Tattoos in Oakley, California, who loves to use passphrases for his passwords. He always cracks me up with the passwords he uses. For example, without giving his passwords away here is an example of what he might use:

ATTCanGoByeBye4Good!!!

By the way, we are using G-rated words in this example, but if you like, you can add non-G-rated words into your passwords. Try to come up with a passphrase that you can relate to so that you or someone else can easily remember the password. Try thinking of common phrases you grew up with, something you say all the time, or something you are known for.

AUTHENTICATION

One of the most recommended security features we have always asked our clients to enable was an extra layer of protection that authenticates your accounts that require any form of log-in credentials.

By adding that extra layer of authentication, each new log-in, will require a form of verification when logging in. Please make sure to always **ENABLE** any form of authentication when possible and available. You will hear authentication terms like:

2FV	2SV	MFA
Two-Factor Verification	Two-Step Verification	Multi-Factor Authentication

Regardless of what it might be called, make sure to inquire with the company, if they supports any form of authentication, because you definitely want to have the extra layer of security in place.

If your account is especially important to you, then you want to make sure they have authentication in place. If they don't support it, then go elsewhere to a company that does support these types of authentication.

AUTH APPS

The most common way to setup your 2FV, 2SV, and MFA is by using your cell phone number to receive a four to eight pin via text. Another common method to authenticate an account is through an "AUTHENTICATOR" app like the ones offered for free by Microsoft or Google Authenticator.

These two apps give you easy, secure access to authenticate your accounts by logging into the app. These apps will generate time-based codes used during an authentication process. We highly recommend that you add an additional PASSCODE, FINGERPRINT, or FACE RECOGNITION to access the Authenticator App on your phone.

BACKUP YOUR ACCOUNTS

WARNING: Make sure to always backup your accounts listed under the authenticator apps because when you get a new phone, even if you do a full restore from the old phone to the new, the accounts in the authenticator app will not transfer over.

OTHER AUTHENTICATION OPTIONS

Backup Codes

In the event your phone stopped working and you can't access the Authenticator App, please make sure to always document, print, or save your "BACKUP CODES" because these codes will serve as a way to verify who you are.

We recommend setting up additional backup steps so you can sign in if other options don't work or are not available.

Backup codes are one-time passcodes that allow you to sign in when you are away from your phone or trying to sign into other computers or devices.

These backup codes are just used to verify who you are when you are signing into your account. This prevents you from entering your main or master password on a device that is not yours. Examples of backup codes:

- Example: x76n-l94v, 281k-cqc5, ljd1-fz2 and will continue with more.
- Example: 4338 1724 3313 1158, 1829 5930 5492 5227 and will continue with more.

Security Keys

A security key is another verification method that allows you to securely sign in. These can be built into your phone, use Bluetooth, or plug directly into your computer's USB port.

PIN

If you are using Google's email services, they, and other companies, offer the ability to have a PIN # to make it easier to sign into Google apps like Roku, Google Admin, and more.

Some products will ask for the pin before you can take any further action. If you enable this option, please choose a strong PIN, and as always avoid using your birthday, address number, or any numbers that relate to you and can be easy to guess. Avoid using simple numbers like 1234 or 9876, or some of the similar common passwords we discussed earlier.

PARTIAL PASSWORDS

One clever strategy, and somewhat technical way to protect your passwords is to only have the browser memorize a part of your password, and when the browser recalls the saved password, you add the additional 3 to 5 characters or whatever you want, towards the end of the password. For example:

> Let's say one of your saved passwords in Google Chrome or Firebox is:
>
> **!WeLoveMicky#1999!**
>
> Have the browser only memorize **!WeLoveMicky#** and each time that you log into your account you will simply click on the pop credentials and the account username and password will automatically populate the with the password **!WeLoveMicky#**, but then you will manually type in the following characters "**1999!**" to complete the entire password.

This partial saving of your passwords protects you from having anyone accessing the password history inside your browsers and obtaining your entire correct passwords. If you already have passwords stored within the Chrome or Firefox browsers, go into the browser's settings to find the list of SAVED passwords and there you will find the website, username, and password list. Next to each line of information there will be an option to COPY, EDIT or REMOVE the password. From there, please edit and delete the desired number of characters at the end of the password. So, the next time you recall the password, it will only enter the partial password.

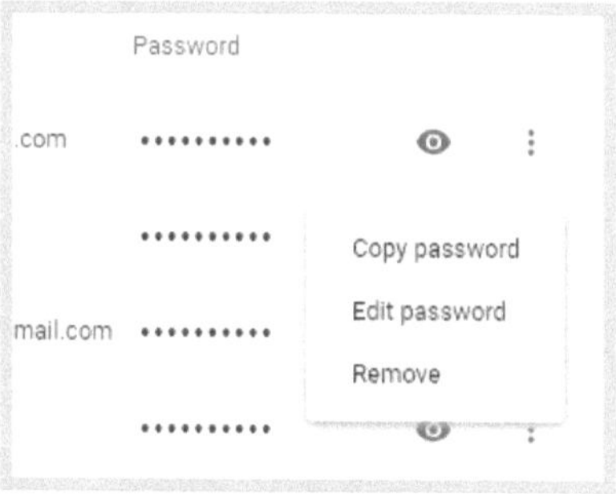

On a side note, several of my clients have allowed these fake support companies or fake IT Specialists, who claim to represent Apple, Google, or Microsoft, to access and hi-jack their computers. Their main goal, and they are very persistent, is to have you download a remote access program like “Anydesk or TeamViewer” in hopes of getting access to your computer and then ask you for your computer log in password.

Since Google Chrome is the most popular browser, the first thing they love to do is get into your Google Chrome settings. Then they click on “Passwords” to view all your accounts and passwords you have stored in Chrome. By using the partial password strategy, it adds an additional layer of protecting your passwords, and it is a good way to prevent anyone (including kids) from knowing your passwords, especially if they have access to your computer.

DISGUISING YOUR PASSWORDS

Our final strategy is disguising your passwords. Disguising your passwords might be something new to you because no one really talks about adding extra characters to your password that don't belong to the password and only make sense to you. Let me explain what I mean by this. Most of my clients like to either save their passwords in:

- Word documents.
- Apple Notes.
- Text themselves the password and save it within their text messages.
- Email it to themselves and store in one of their email subfolders.
- Write it on a piece of paper. Yes, I have seen so many clients go as far as writing their password on a piece of paper and having the paper tucked away somewhere around their computer or desk.

If you must or plan on having some physical form to remind you of your password, we highly recommend disguising your passwords. Here are two examples of what we mean.

The FRONT & BACK example

Let's say your password is: **Cali89&Bill76.** Instead of saving, typing, texting, emailing, or writing your password as Cali89&Bill76. You can disguise the password as:

DogCali89&Bill767575

Where you can pick the X number of characters you want to place in the **FRONT** and **BACK** of your password; for this example, we used "**Dog**" on the front and "**7575**" on the back. The "**Dog7575**" will be the characters only known by you or the person you share it with that aren't actually part of the password.

The FRONT, MIDDLE, & BACK example

Let's say your password is: **!LoveBMXin89!.** Instead of saving, typing, texting, emailing, or writing your password as !LoveBMXin89!. You can disguise the password as:

Nor!LoveCalBMXin89!21

Where you can pick the X number of characters you want to place in the **FRONT, MIDDLE** and **BACK** of your password; for this example, we used "**Nor**" on the front, used "**Cal**" in the middle, and "**21**" on the back. The "**NorCal21**" will be characters only known by you or the person you share it with.

NAKED PASSWORDS

We have always told our clients to never **leave your password naked** out in the open where people can see it. Make sure to dress it up and disguise it with some other characters that are only known by you and are not part of the actual password. Another simple way to disguise your passwords is to consider using the following special characters to replace some of the letters in your passwords:

$ instead of an S	1 instead of an L
+ instead of T	@ instead of A

If someone does find your disguised passwords, they might try to figure out the disguised password or use different password combinations, but eventually the account will be locked. You might even receive an email letting you know that your account has been locked out because of so many failed attempts.

Disguising your password is just another way to avoid making it too easy for someone to get into your accounts. Please protect your accounts and passwords with the strategies that work best for you.

While doing some research on password hacking, I came across this very interesting table of the max time it takes to break a password. As you can see the more mix of characters you have in your password, the longer it takes to break it.

PASSWORD DIFFICULTY

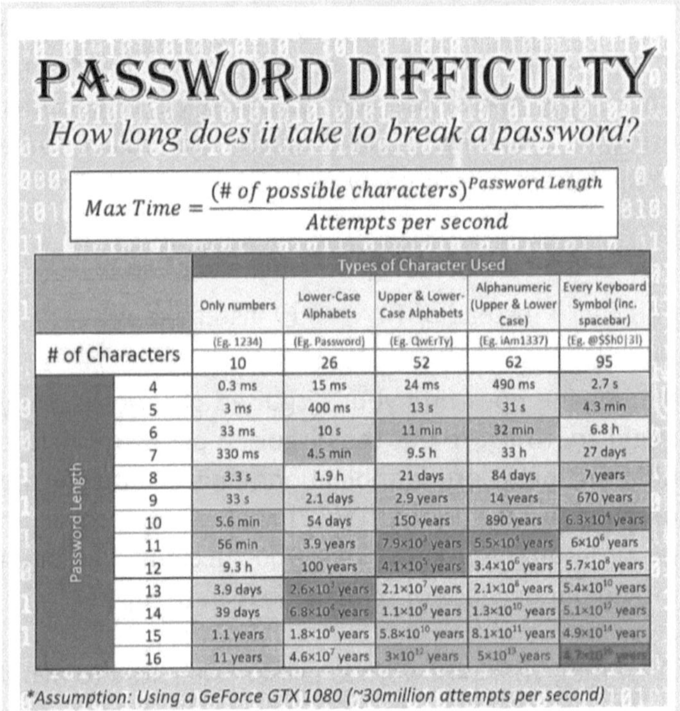

PASSWORD DIFFICULTY

How long does it take to break a password?

$$Max\ Time = \frac{(\#\ of\ possible\ characters)^{Password\ Length}}{Attempts\ per\ second}$$

		Types of Character Used				
		Only numbers	Lower-Case Alphabets	Upper & Lower-Case Alphabets	Alphanumeric (Upper & Lower Case)	Every Keyboard Symbol (inc. spacebar)
# of Characters		(Eg. 1234) 10	(Eg. Password) 26	(Eg. QwErTy) 52	(Eg. iAm1337) 62	(Eg. @$Sh0|3l) 95
Password Length	4	0.3 ms	15 ms	24 ms	490 ms	2.7 s
	5	3 ms	400 ms	13 s	31 s	4.3 min
	6	33 ms	10 s	11 min	32 min	6.8 h
	7	330 ms	4.5 min	9.5 h	33 h	27 days
	8	3.3 s	1.9 h	21 days	84 days	7 years
	9	33 s	2.1 days	2.9 years	14 years	670 years
	10	5.6 min	54 days	150 years	890 years	6.3×10^4 years
	11	56 min	3.9 years	7.9×10^3 years	5.5×10^4 years	6×10^6 years
	12	9.3 h	100 years	4.1×10^5 years	3.4×10^6 years	5.7×10^8 years
	13	3.9 days	2.6×10^3 years	2.1×10^7 years	2.1×10^8 years	5.4×10^{10} years
	14	39 days	6.8×10^4 years	1.1×10^9 years	1.3×10^{10} years	5.1×10^{12} years
	15	1.1 years	1.8×10^6 years	5.8×10^{10} years	8.1×10^{11} years	4.9×10^{14} years
	16	11 years	4.6×10^7 years	3×10^{12} years	5×10^{13} years	4.7×10^{16} years

**Assumption: Using a GeForce GTX 1080 (~30million attempts per second)*

Picture curiosity from the University of South Wales

PASSWORD SECRETS NOTEBOOK SAMPLES

1	ACCOUNTS AND PASSWORDS	A

Name
Account Type

Username
Current PW

Date
Previous PWS

Email used
Phone Used

Auth Enable
Auth used:

PW Name
Auth app Passcode
Pin #

Secrete Questions & Answers (Keywords)
Notes

CHAPTER

3

EMAIL ADDRESSES & SETTINGS

DIFFERENT EMAIL ADDRESSES

In addition to protecting your accounts with strong passwords, we also highly recommend having different email addresses for different purposes and based on importance. By having different email addresses, it allows for another layer of protection for all your accounts.

One time we had a client who was very hesitant in creating an online/cloud storage service account like Dropbox, Google Drive, or OneDrive. His goal was to create a better way to store his files locally and have all his files synchronize between his computers, smartphone, and devices. Most of his data included personal files, pictures, and some business files. Dropbox was the chosen option, but to ease his worries and improve the max protection possible, we:

First, we created a brand-new email address to ONLY be used for Dropbox. The reason for this was he had publicly given his main email address out to too many people and was already logged into too many other online accounts.

Second, we enabled all the security features that were available from Dropbox such as:

- **His Cell #**: Authentication via text.
- **His Wife's Cell #**: We added his wife's phone number as a backup (this was optional) but if he

were to lose access to his primary security code source, Dropbox can send the codes to the backup number instead. Once again, this is optional, but we do recommend you consider setting up a backup phone number in case your cell phone is lost or stops working or you are unable to receive your security code.

- **One-Time Backup Codes**: We printed and saved the one-time backup codes special only to his Dropbox account.
- **Security Keys**: We did not enable this security feature because he did not like the idea of using a USB drive to store the security keys.

Third, we implemented the THUMB Finger type of super-duper strong password by using the max of 30 characters. This new email address was to ONLY be used for his Dropbox, online/cloud storage account and he was NOT to promote or give the email address to anyone, except for his wife of course.

Earlier we mentioned that passwords are the first line of defense, however, we at TekkieTeks sometimes go back and forth debating that we feel that having an email address that no one knows and is used for only important accounts, can also be considered the first line of defense. So, maybe your email address is your first line of defense and your password is your second line of defense. Your thoughts are welcome.

One way to help you understand the different email addresses we recommend is, we have categorized them as **Important, Noncritical, Fun,** and **Alias** email addresses. Before we jump into the four email addresses, let me first provide you with an explanation of what an alias email is, since it is the most complicated of four.

EMAIL ALIAS

WHAT IS AN EMAIL ALIAS?

One way to think of an email alias is to think of it like a toll-free number, a toll-free number is used to PROTECT or HIDE your cell or business number from being advertised. Plus, toll-free numbers help avoid getting your number on the spammer's list of numbers. So, when someone calls a toll-free number, it gets forwarded to the number you desired.

An email alias works the same way, it forwards the email message sent to the alias to your primary email address, such as our important, noncritical, and fun email addresses. An alias email is a good way to **disguise** your email address.

Keep in mind that everything sent to the alias email address is received into your primary inbox. Alias emails can also help differentiate a single email account without having to pay for multiple inboxes. Most importantly, if your alias email is receiving tons of spam messages, it would be much easier to just delete the alias email address and start a new one, rather than it unsubscribe to all the spam messages.

You cannot REPLY to an email alias, if you reply to an alias message, you will be providing them with your primary email address. Which is fine in some cases, but always double check which email you are using when sending your emails, especially when it comes to your important email.

We have always recommended to our clients to use an email alias to keep their Important emails protected and minimize the amount of spam. In fact, we have a client, who has used her Important Business email address for:

- Both her Important Business and Personal accounts
- Her Noncritical business accounts
- All of her Fun personal accounts

She now gets over 300 spam emails a day.

In comparisons to my important business email address, I maybe get one to three spam email messages a week.

From the start of my business, I strictly used my important email address ONLY FOR CLIENTS who I met personally. My alias email addresses receive most of the company junk. Once I get about 50 spam messages a day, I simply delete it and start a new one, because it is much easier for me to just DELETE MY EMAIL ALIAS THAN IT IS TO UNSUBSCRIBE FROM EACH SPAM email. Please, always use an email alias to protect your other email addresses, especially your important email addresses. It is also worth mentioning that alias emails are also considered to be disposable email addresses. We recommend using email alias mostly for:

- App/software trials
- Attending free events like webinars or networking meetings
- Testing or demoing a product
- First time Zoom meetings
- Experimenting to see if the person or vendor is a good fit to work with

The goal of the alias is to protect your important and noncritical emails. If this sounds confusing, which it can be, feel free to call us or setup a free consultation with TekkieTeks.

EMAIL ADDRESSES

Now that we talked about email alias, let's dive into having and how to use the following types of email addresses personally and professionally:

Important	Noncritical	Fun

To ease in the understanding, we have organized it into two categories: Business and Personal email addresses. Each table below will have the type of email address, who we feel you can share it with, examples of each type of email address, and a brief explanation on how to use that type of email.

An email is broken up into three parts:		
Username	@	Email Domain Name

For the sake of our email address examples we will be using:

- Username as John Doe
- Company name as CompanyABC to protect our company emails
- DomainABC to protect all related email addresses associated with email service providers such as Apple using iCloud.com, Google using Gmail.com, Microsoft using Outlook.com, and Protonmail using Protonmail.com.

IMPORTANT <u>BUSINESS</u> EMAIL ADDRESSES (IBEA)

IBEA are typically broken down by using some arrangement of your name followed by your company email domain name. All IBEA should be strictly used for anything that is especially important to your business, which is mostly communicating with your bank, financial business accounts, and existing clients.

Keep in mind, that sometimes when you meet a new potential client it doesn't mean that you should provide them with your IBEA. Please, <u>filter</u> all new clients (prospects) first before you provide them with your IBEA.

If new clients do ask for an email address, please provide them with the Noncritical Email Address first (see below) and once they have become a solid and trustworthy client, then proceed communicating with them using your IBEA. By filtering your clients first, it will help keep your IBEA clean and have less spam in the future.

Your main goal here is to always **PROTECT** your IBEA at all times. Because once you start promoting your IBEA to your clients, it will be very difficult to change your IBEA later on and letting your clients know of the new changes is a lengthy process.

Some clients will take a long time to update their records of your new email change. In fact, we have some clients who still have our very first email address, compunerd@jps.com that we started using when we first started back in 1999. It is no longer active but when we service their computers, we update their records for them.

With all IBEA, you will have to pay a monthly fee to obtain an IBEA for your company and all IBEA do provide a greater level of security and protection. See examples below.

TYPE	**IBEA**
SHARE WITH	**EXAMPLES**
Financial Account and Clients Only	John@CompanyABC.com
	John.Doe@CompanyABC.com
	JohnD@CompanyABC.com
	JDoe@CompanyABC.com

NONCRITICAL BUSINESS EMAIL ADDRESSES (NBEA)

NBEA are typically broken down by using some arrangement of whatever you want as the username, but when it comes to your NBEA we recommend using your company name as the username. Then selecting the email service provider that has your company name available.

With so many people using Gmail, iCloud, and Outlook, you will find it sometimes very difficult to grab an email address with your company name as the username. For TekkieTeks, we were lucky to grab **TekkieTeks@gmail.com**. If you have a common username for your company or it has been taken, then proceed with another email service provider until you find an email address with your company name. **Goal here is to get your username to have your company name.**

NBEA addresses are fairly easy to create, and you do not have to pay a monthly fee unless you need the additional services offered by the companies. NBEA by companies:

- Apple, their email domain name is iCloud.com or me.com or mac.com.
- Google, their email domain name is Gmail.com.

- Microsoft, their email domain is Outlook.com, Hotmail.com, or Live.com.
- Protonmail, their email domain name is just Protonmail.

We recommend using NBEA for all non-client related activities such as your:

- Affiliates' accounts
- Business website
- Distributors' accounts
- IRS purposes
- Online purchases related to your company
- Vendors' communications

In a nutshell, you will pretty much use NBEA addresses for any non-client communication activities. See the examples below.

TYPE	NBEA
SHARE WITH	**EXAMPLES**
Vendors or Distributors Online Biz Purchases	CompanyABC@gmail.com
	CompanyABC@iCloud.com
	CompanyABC@Outlook.com
	CompanyABC@Protonmail.com

ALIAS BUSINESS EMAIL ADDRESSES (ABEA)

We already went into great details about alias email addresses. Here are some examples of ABEA.

TYPE	ABEA
SHARE WITH	**EXAMPLES**
New Clients, Vendors, New Companies & Your Company Website	Support@CompanyABC.com
	Info@CompanyABC.com
	Sales@CompanyABC.com
	SocialMedia4TT@domainABC.com
	WeTekkieNerds@domainABC.com

IMPORTANT PERSONAL EMAIL ADDRESSES (IPEA)

Similar to important business email addresses, your IPEA relates to what is very important to you on the personal side. See examples that we have used in the past.

With IPEA, you are not to share with anyone for the exception of your spouse or maybe your parents. The IPEA is to only be used for communications related to your personal financial accounts, banking, credit cards, PayPal, investments, or what you consider to be *VERY IMPORTANT* to you personally.

The goal here is not to MIX your IPEA with your fun email addresses (see FPEA explanation), and by keeping them separate, it will make it more difficult for someone to guess what your username is for any important account. Our top companies we recommend for IPEA are:

iCloud.com, Gmail.com, Outlook.com, and Protonmail.com

Most of our clients have used their first and last name with their IPEA. Back in the early years, it was ok to do so and we recommended using their **first name or full name**. Nowadays, you are welcome to continue to use your first and last name, but as of 2000, we have been recommending to not use your first and last name, instead create an email that has nothing related to your name. See examples below.

TYPE	**IPEA**
SHARE WITH	**EXAMPLES**
Spouse and/or Parents	Financial4TeamZ@domainABC.com
	Money4TeamZ@domainABC.com
	RetireB42050@domainABC.com
	OurZKidsMoney@domainABC.com

FUN PERSONAL EMAIL ADDRESSES (FPEA)

Similar to noncritical business email addresses (NBEA), your FPEA relate to what is NOT important to you on the personal side. Get creative with your fun personal email addresses. FPEA will be strictly used for everything and everyone else that is not part of the important emails. You can create whatever username you want, but avoid using your full name, any words like sexy, 69, hot, mama, big, or XXX. You will get a lot of spam from porn companies. FPEA will be strictly used for entertainment such as:

- Communicating between your friends, family, the kid's schools, and sports program.
- For joke related emails and Social Media sites.
- Signing up for the gym membership and any form of subscriptions.
- Medical/doctor related

TYPE	**FPEA**
SHARE WITH	**EXAMPLES**
Friends, Family, Social Media, or Everything else	Be creative and create whatever email you want.

ALIAS PERSONAL EMAIL ADDRESSES (APEA)

Like the business alias, use personal alias to protect your important and fun personal email addresses. Use personal alias for trials, free events, webinars, testing or demoing a product, and first time zoom meetings.

TYPE	**APEA**
SHARE WITH	**EXAMPLES**
Free, Trials, New Events, Testing a product or if you are unsure in buying	BnJnGnMnL@domainABC.com
	LoveMyLife4Ever@domainABC.com
	BBallRuns89@domainABC.com
	Dogs143Cats@domainABC.com

ALL EMAIL ADDRESSES

As mentioned before with passwords, with email addresses make sure to also enable the following when possible:

- **ALWAYS** turn on or enable their Authentication options.
- **ALWAYS** assign App Specific Password to your applications or devices.
- **ALWAYS** save, print, or store your Recover Codes

CLOSING OR DELETING EMAIL ACCOUNTS

When closing or deleting old or unused email accounts make sure to first **backup** and then delete all email messages, folders, contacts, notes, and then empty the trash. Then follow it up in about 30 days to make sure the trash was deleted, and nothing is left behind. Then proceed to closing your email account.

Never leave an old or unused email account open.

EMAIL SETTINGS

When it came to email addresses, the most common question we received from our clients was related to the email SERVER SETTINGS for their various email addresses. Please search online or contact your email provider to obtain your email server settings. Please make sure to document the settings in the password secrets notebook for each different email address. For example, if you use Google, your typically server settings will look like:

POP	pop.gmail.com
PORT numbers for POP is 995	

IMAP	imap.gmail.com
PORT numbers for IMAP 993	

SMTP	smtp.gmail.com
PORT numbers for SMTP are 25, 465 or 567	

MICROSOFT EXCHANGE OR GOOGLE G-SUITE

We would like to touch on a trend we have seen over the years, where many of our residential clients have been moving over to using business email services such as Microsoft Exchange or Google G-Suite.

Please research both Microsoft's Exchange and Google's G-Suite to determine which one will work for you personally and/or professionally. We have used both in our own company and with many of our clients. If we had to help you pick or recommend one to you, we can say that the winner will be Microsoft Exchange.

WHAT IT IS MICROSOFT EXCHANGE?

Microsoft Hosted Exchange is an alternative email, calendar, contact list and task list. If you are an iPhone user, it's like Apple's iCloud. However, Microsoft Exchange works with any or all devices and has always worked for us with no down time. We have used G-Suite, but it was too basic for us and we continue to use Microsoft Exchange.

The benefits of Microsoft Hosted Exchange are the following:

- It is one central location for all your business emails, calendar, contacts, and tasks.

- It is more productive, efficient, and offers more security than your local Outlook.
- You can access your email through Microsoft Outlook on your desktop or laptop, Outlook Web Access, tablets, and mobile devices. Every device will have the same email list, calendars appointments, contacts information, and tasks list. This prevents email duplications like other types of email management systems.
- You can create and share multiple calendars for you and your staff.
- Task management allows you to create and delegate tasks.
- If offers e-mail filtering, encryption, archiving and recovery. This allows you and your company to use Outlook to communicate with minimal risk.
- Offers real-time anti-spam and virus defenses.
- It prevents a virus outbreak before it reaches your network.
- Efficient way of backing up the emails because it's not stored locally on your computer, but stores on company's server who helps on recovering your Outlook information during a crash.

SETUP

When it comes to saving your Microsoft Exchange server settings, it's best to log into your Microsoft account to copy and paste the server settings within your hosting company. Please talk to your hosting support company to understand how to configure them.

VERY IMPORTANT

Make sure to document the email and password for your Exchange account in the password secrets notebook.

Make sure to back up your Exchange mailbox at least every 3 to 6 months by exporting your PST file and password protect the exported PST file.

PASSWORD SECRETS NOTEBOOK SAMPLES

IMPORTANT	EMAIL ADDRESS AND SETTINGS

POP IMAP SMTP

Incoming Port # Outgoing Port #

Username/eMail PW

Auth Enable ☐ 2FV ☐ 2SV ☐ MFA Auth used: ☐ SMS ☐ Auth App ☐ Back up codes ☐ Security Key

Phone # Used for SMS

	App or Device Name	App Specific PW		App or Device Name	App Specific PW
1			5		
2			6		
3			7		
4			8		

Alias 1

Codes Alias 2

Alias 3

Important eMail Address (IF) Compromised Info

Compromised on Changed PW to

Closed eMail on Because

NONCRITICAL EMAIL ADDRESS AND SETTINGS

POP IMAP SMTP

Incoming Port # Outgoing Port #

Username/eMail PW

Auth Enable ☐ 2FV ☐ 2SV ☐ MFA Auth used: ☐ SMS ☐ Auth App ☐ Back up codes ☐ Security Key

Phone # Used for SMS

	App or Device Name	App Specific PW		App or Device Name	App Specific PW
1			5		
2			6		
3			7		
4			8		

Codes

Alias 1

Alias 2

Alias 3

Noncritical eMail Address (IF) Compromised Info

Compromised on Changed PW to

Closed eMail on Because

FUN	EMAIL ADDRESS AND SETTINGS

POP

IMAP

SMTP

Incoming Port #

Outgoing Port #

Username/eMail

PW

Auth Enable ☐ 2FV ☐ 2SV ☐ MFA Auth used: ☐ SMS ☐ Auth App ☐ Back up codes ☐ Security Key

Phone # Used for SMS

	App or Device Name	App Specific PW		App or Device Name	App Specific PW
1			5		
2			6		
3			7		
4			8		

Codes

Alias 1

Alias 2

Alias 3

Fun eMail Address (IF) Compromised Info

Compromised on

Changed PW to

Closed eMail on

Because

EXCHANGE EMAIL ADDRESS AND SETTINGS

eMail PW

Auth Enable ☐ 2FV ☐ 2SV ☐ MFA Phone # Used for SMS

Alias 1 Alias 2

Alias 3 Alias 4

Login URL

Exchange eMail Address (IF) Compromised Info

Compromised on Changed PW to

Closed eMail on Because

Outlook "PST" Files History of Exports & Backups

Dates exported & PST backup	Name of PST File	Password used (optional)

Save PST to Cloud Drive ☐ OneDrive, ☐ Google Drive, ☐ DropBox, ☐ Box, or ☐ Other____________

Save PST to External Drive ☐ USB Drive ☐ External Drive, or ☐ Other ________________________

Save PST to another Internal Drive ☐ D Drive, ☐ E Drive or ☐ Other _________________________

CHAPTER

4

COMPUTERS, SMARTPHONES, & DEVICES

Protecting all your computers, smartphones, and devices are just as important as protecting your accounts. We will only be focusing on Mac and Windows computers (desktops and laptops) and iPhones.

WINDOWS LOCAL VS EMAIL ACCOUNT

When it comes to configuring your Windows login profile, you have two options. You can either set it up as a local account (similar to the first versions from Windows 98 to Windows 7) or you can set it up with an email account; sometimes called Microsoft Account.

When deciding which type of Windows login profile to pick, it comes down to a matter of preference. However, most clients are not aware that you can still configure your Windows login profile similar to the older versions of Windows. Microsoft pushes for users to create an email account because of the many benefits and features they offer, but again it's not for everyone.

Please research the two types of Windows login profiles by searching "Which is better local or email (Microsoft) account."

We have always recommended that our clients create a local account over an email account. Mainly because local accounts are local and not tied to any email address. Depending on the email address there is a higher probability that your email can get hacked and changing an email account is more work versus setting up a local account.

Quick way to setup a Local Account on a new Windows computer
When configuring your new computer, connect all the cables, with the exception of your ethernet cable. You will plug it in after your local user profile is created. Please turn on the PC and then proceed through the steps until you reach connect to your network or Wi-Fi. Please <u>DO NOT CONNECT ADD</u> Wi-Fi and continue to leave your ethernet unplugged. Located at bottom left corner, click "**Skip for Now**" and follow the next steps. This will quickly allow you to create a Local Account. After you entered your password, you will arrive at your Windows desktop, at this point is when you add your Wi-Fi credentials or plug in your ethernet cable to have internet access.

If you decide to use an email account please make sure to use either your "noncritical business" or "fun personal" type of email address. Regardless which

Windows login profile you use, please make sure to use an **index finger password** for this type of account.

Please document the username for the local account and the email address for the email account in your password secrets notebook.

BIOS PASSWORDS

Most people have never heard of or are not aware that you can also add an additional layer of password protection to your Windows computer right before you get to your Windows login screen.

A BIOS password is an extra layer of protection to prevent someone from booting up your computer pass the BIOS phase (before the Windows' log in screen).

This BIOS password adds a layer of security that locks the early stages of the startup process in your Windows computers. Once you have entered the BIOS' password, the boot cycle will continue as normal to get you to enter your Windows login profile password.

To add a password to your BIOS, we recommend researching your computer model's steps on how to enter into your BIOS to add the BIOS password to your computer.

Most manufactures use either the F2 or F12 to get into your BIOS as the computer is booting up.

Be aware that if you forget your BIOS password, it is going to be a little difficult to reset the password yourself.

Please document the BIOS password in your password secrets notebook so that you do not forget the password. In the event you will have to reset it, you will need a technician to reset it for you. Make sure they know what they are doing because not many know how to reset these types of passwords.

MAC COMPUTERS

With all Mac computers, you simply follow the instructions by providing your username and password. In the event you forgot your password you can simply reset it using your Apple ID. In some cases, it can be a process for most people, so it is faster to just document your password in the password secrets notebook.

GUEST USER ACCOUNTS FOR MACS

If you have kids or guests who use your Mac computer, we strongly suggest not sharing your password or user profile. Instead we recommend enabling the "**GUEST**" user account on your Mac. A guest account does not require a password which is prefect to protect your password.

A guest user account allows for anyone like your friends and family members to have access to your Mac computer and is a protective way to share your computer without them having access to your personal user account or files. This prevents them from deleting anything by mistake or wandering around your profile and making changes.

One of the most common problems we get from our clients is when they allowed someone into their profile and the user made some of sort of changes to their files, screen, and profile. Some have even deleted all the files on their desktop. We have to come in and undo what the user just did. Things were added, misplaced, or deleted and the profile just wasn't the same after they used it.

One recommendation we will suggest is to always enable or turn on the Guest user account around the holidays so that you can allow friends and family to use your computer. Just make sure to log out of your profile and log them into the Guest account.

WARNING: When a guest logs out of your computer, all the information such as files, stored passwords, browser history/cookies, and all downloads they added to your Mac computer will be deleted the minute you log out of the Guest account.

STANDARD USER PROFILE FOR WINDOWS

For creating a Guest profile on Windows computers, you will need to create a "**STANDARD**" local user (not an email) account which allows them to only have "standard" permissions versus administration or full access to your Windows computer. Once you create it, you now have the option to leave it for future guests or just delete it manually to erase what they loaded on the Guest profile. Windows Guest profiles are not like the Mac Guest profiles. You have to delete then create this type of user profile again or each time.

PHONES

- Keep phones secure
- Place Lock on Phone. Change your phone's passcode ever so often.
- Update your devices and software.
- Charge your phone to 100% and use it until it reaches 5% and recharge it. Helps save the battery.
- Avoid jail breaking (or rooting) your phone or side-loading apps.
- When it comes to adding fingerprints and face recognition, make sure to also add your spouse's fingerprints and face recognition in event they need to get access to your phone.

ENCRYPTION FOR WINDOWS

We have always recommended our clients encrypt their computers, especially LAPTOPS since they are portable and easier to lose or steal. When it comes to buying a Windows computer, we direct our clients to purchase a computer that comes with Windows **Professional** 64-bit. Windows Pro includes BitLocker.

What is BitLocker:

- BitLocker is a full volume encryption with Windows **Professional** versions. BitLocker is designed to protect data by providing encryption for entire C Drive and other type of drives.
- In the event you purchased a computer with Windows Home Edition, give us a call or talk to your local IT Support Specialist on the options to encrypting your hard drive.
- To it yourself and save you some money on hiring someone like TekkieTeks, you have the option to go to Microsoft.com directly and purchase an upgraded license to Windows Professional. Then enable BitLocker.

ENCRYPTION FOR MACS

All Mac computers come standard with "**FileVault**" to easily encrypt your hard drive. Here are the steps:

- Go to the little Apple on the top right corner
- Then click on System Preferences
- Then click on Security & Privacy
- Then click on FileVault
- Then unlock the lock located on the bottom left corner of the Security & Privacy windows
- Then click Turn On FileVault

With all encryptions, make sure to keep your encryption password protected and safe. We also recommend to always encrypt your External and USB drives. Encrypting your data on any of your removable storage devices can make it more difficult for anyone to have access to your data on your device if it becomes lost or stolen. Encrypting your hard drive does take some time, please do so after you are done using your computer.

RECOMMENDATIONS

- Always keep up and install your operating system updates for both the Mac and Windows computers.
- Always "Sleep" or "Turn off" your computer if you are going to be gone for more than three hours.
- **Lock your smartphone and tablet devices**.
- Set your device to automatically lock after a period of inactivity.
- Disable Bluetooth when you're not using it.
- Put your phone on Airplane mode every night before going to bed.
- Every quarter, review your list of programs on your computers and Apps on your devices and if you have not used them in a while, please delete or uninstall them.
- Delete and reinstall your most used Apps like Facebook, TikTok, or Instagram every three months to help with your device's memory. By deleting these apps, it will help clear some of the "**Other**" memory on your phones. Once you have deleted them, you can reinstall them.
- When you purchase a new device such as a Mac computer or iPhone, if you plan to give your old computer or phone away, make sure to log into **www.AppleID.Apple.com** to find the old computer and devices to delete them off your Apple ID account.

- Install antivirus and malware software on your computers and devices (if they support it).
- Make it a monthly routine to always backup your files.

If you have questions regarding anything in this chapter, book, or the recommendations above, feel free to reach out to us at **www.TekkieTeks.com**.

PASSWORD SECRETS NOTEBOOK SAMPLES

COMPUTER 1 NAME

☐ Mac ☐ Windows ☐ Desktop ☐ Laptop ☐ Personal ☐ Business ☐ Kids ☐ Other ___________

Account Created on Local/Email Account

PW Used Hint Used

BIOS' PW Computer Name

Mac Guest Accounts Enabled ☐ Yes ☐ No
"FileVault" Enabled on my Mac ☐ Yes ☐ No

Windows Standard Accounts Created ☐ Yes ☐ No
"BitLocker" Enable on the Windows Pro ☐ Yes ☐ No

#	Windows Security Questions	Answers
1		
2		
3		

SMARTPHONES AND OTHER DEVICES

Type of Phone ☐ iPhone ☐ Android ☐ Other ____________________ Passcode

Apple ID or Google ID PW

Enabled ☐ PIN ☐ My Fingerprint ☐ Spouse Fingerprint ☐ Face Recognition ☐ Other ____________

Primary Phone # Used

CHAPTER

5

DOCS, SOFTWARE, APPS, & LICENSES

DOCUMENTS

Many of our clients were not aware of or didn't know how to secure their important documents. In fact, many of our clients will use Microsoft Excel or Word to save their passwords. But the problem was that these documents were not password protected. If you plan to store all your passwords in an Excel or Word document, please make sure to password protect these documents and prevent someone from opening or editing these documents.

Microsoft allows you to easily add passwords to protect your documents from being open or making changes by someone else. For example, in Word you want to look for "**Protect Document**" and then select encrypt it with a password. Now, each time that you open the Word document, it will require a password.

One last thing, when it comes to password protecting your documents, please do not NAME your document with any association with the word "**password**" or the letters PWS. Name your password document like Home Recipes, Home Plants, or HS Reunion. You get the idea, name it so that it prevents someone from trying to get access to your password document. Please, make sure to back up your password document on a monthly basis and as a backup please print or document your password in your password secrets notebook.

SOFTWARE

When it comes to apps and software programs, please document the username and password in your password secrets notebook right away or the minute you have finished setting up the accounts. In addition to your usernames and passwords, we also have found it very important to document the following information related to apps and software programs:

- App/Software
- Purchased date, the cost, and order number
- Last 4 of credit card
- License or Serial number or Product Key Codes
- Technical Support number
- Username with the associated password
- Subscription: No number of months or years
- Devices with installed software and the number of users and devices.

For example, QuickBooks and Quicken have been the two programs many of our clients have forgotten their password to. In order to reset their passwords, we had to purchase additional software from Intuit to hack and remove the password.

SUBSCRIPTIONS

Subscriptions have become a common business model for most app and software companies but has become a frustrating situation for many of our clients, which we have experienced first-hand. This is one of the reasons why we created the password secrets book/notebook and where the idea was created.

From our experience, most clients do not keep track of the number of subscriptions they sign up to, or the costs associated with each subscription, and they end up paying for similar monthly or yearly subscriptions. Sometimes these subscription charges repeat two to four times per year. Some clients thought that this was normal.

For example, we had one client where he was being charged three times a year for the same type of anti-virus protection. He had no idea, he thought that those were normal charges. Please keep track of all your subscriptions, document the following in your password secrets notebook:

- The App or Software Name and Version #.
- The License or Serial # so that you can compare it if you get repeated charges.
- The Order # to easily recall the purchase to speak to their billing department.
- The Username and Password to the subscription.

- Know the # of months or years for the Subscription and the # of licenses for each of your devices.
- Please list devices with the subscription.
- The last four digits of your credit card. You will find that some of these subscription companies will sometimes not list your credit card information.

Please, if you no longer plan on ever using a paid subscription, delete and/or close the account so that your email is no longer associated with that account. Remove or delete your credit card, as well. We have seen companies recharge or reactivate an old account.

CLOSED ALL UNUSED ACCOUNTS

RENEWALS (TURN THEM OFF)

You should always be IN CHARGE of knowing when you will be CHARGED with any type of subscription. We highly recommend to **ALWAYS TURN OFF THE AUTO RENEWALS**. Auto renewals have become a nightmare for many clients.

PASSWORD SECRETS NOTEBOOK SAMPLES

DOCUMENTS			
1	Name	Purpose of Doc	
	Password	Doc Type	
2	Name	Purpose of Doc	
	Password	Doc Type	
3	Name	Purpose of Doc	
	Password	Doc Type	
4	Name	Purpose of Doc	
	Password	Doc Type	
5	Name	Purpose of Doc	
	Password	Doc Type	
6	Name	Purpose of Doc	
	Password	Doc Type	
7	Name	Purpose of Doc	
	Password	Doc Type	
8	Name	Purpose of Doc	
	Password	Doc Type	
9	Name	Purpose of Doc	
	Password	Doc Type	
10	Name	Purpose of Doc	
	Password	Doc Type	

SOFTWARE AND APPS

Name Date Cost

Order # Credit Card Auto Renewal ☐ Turned Off

Tech Support # License or Serial #

Username PW

Subscription ☐ Yes or ☐ No # of months or years? # of Users/Devices

Computers, Smart Phones or Devices with software installed

Name Date Cost

Order # Credit Card Auto Renewal ☐ Turned Off

Tech Support # License or Serial #

Username PW

Subscription ☐ Yes or ☐ No # of months or years? # of Users/Devices

Computers, Smart Phones or Devices with software installed

CHAPTER

6

YOUR ISP, WIRELESS NETWORK, & IoT DEVICES

INTERNET SERVICE PROVIDER (ISP)

When it comes to your Internet Service Provider (ISP) such as ATT, CenturyLink, Comcast (Xfinity), Cox, DirecTV, and many others depending on where you live, what we have learned when working with our clients and dealing with ISP is making sure you have your ISP's:

NAME AND YOUR ACCOUNT NUMBER

Make sure they have YOU listed with your correct name. Know all account number associated with your ISP. Sometimes the account number on your bill will be different than the account they have on your file.

THE TOLL-FREE PHONE NUMBER TO REACH SUPPORT

Document and find the most direct or best phone number to reach your ISP quickly.

Many times, the toll-free number on the ISP's website is different for their billing and support number. Once you have found the best phone number, please document it in your password secrets notebook. This way, you are not spending time looking for it.

DATE AND PROMISED SPEEDS (MBPS)

When you activate your internet service, make sure to document the date your service started. Most importantly, know what your actual DOWNLOAD and UPLOAD speeds are versus depending on what the ISP provided you.

Most ISP focus on how great their download speeds are but never mention their upload speeds. Please go to **https://speedtest.xfinity.com** or search for "Internet Speed Test" and you will find several tools out there to help you know your actual download and upload speeds.

Make sure to check on your speeds every so often to make sure you are paying for what the ISP promised you on the day your signed up for their service.

For example, my average download speed is between 95 to 100 Mbps and my upload speed is between 9 to 12 Mbps.

FEES

Knowing, monitoring, and comparing your current fees is very important. Many ISPs will slowly increase their fees without your knowledge. It might be a few unnoticeable dollars here and there, please document in your password secrets notebook your initial fees and stay on top of it. If the price does go up, give your ISP a call to understand the price increase.

YOUR IP ADDRESS

An Internet Protocol (IP) address is like your driver's license to go on the Internet. IP addresses give away your location and is used to monitor your online activity.

This might not be a big deal, but after receiving many calls from our clients about why a certain number was showing up on some sites and their emails, we started educating our clients on how to find their own IP address that was assigned by their ISP.

To find what your IP Address, simply go to **www.MyIPaddress.com** and document the number in your password secrets notebook for future reference if you ever need to compare your IP Address.

We recommend hiding your IP address by using some form of Virtual Private Network (VPN) service either on your router or per computer or device. Research what a VPN is to determine if it is something you might need.

All this is can be somewhat tekkie, please reach out to us and we will be happy to explain.

ROUTER

DEFAULT IP ADDRESS

When it comes to understanding your router, it's important to know your router's Gateway IP address so that you have the power to make the necessary changes to your router. From our experience, many of the ISP don't provide their clients with the:

- IP address to the router
- Router's login information such as username and password.

Before the ISP technician leaves your house, make sure to obtain all the necessary router's login information. Please use the password secrets notebook's "Router Factory Default Settings" shown below to document the appropriate information.

ROUTER FACTORY DEFAULT SETTINGS

By default, every router will come with their own default IP address, such as:

- 192.168.**1**.1 or 192.168.**0**.1
- 10.0.**0**.1 or 10.0.**1**.1

Make sure to ask the technician for the default router IP address. Your router will come with a default USERNAME of "**Admin**" and chances are that you will not be able to change the default username. However, if it is possible to change, we recommend using a different username.

Your router will have a default password of "**password**" and yes, they use the word password as the password. It's important to know and document the router's factory default password so that you can reset your router and apply your own credentials.

YOUR NEW ROUTER SETTINGS

After the technician has provided and left your house, please make sure to log into the router using your browser (Chrome, Edge, or Firefox) to make the necessary changes.

Please change the default IP address of the router from like 192.168.**1**.1 to 192.168.**250**.1. Next, make changes to your username if possible and change the default password. Please document the new username and password in your password secrets notebook.

ROUTER FIRMWARE

Every three months log into your router to make sure you have installed the latest **FIRMWARE**, which is the built-in software for your router or specific hardware.

WIRELESS NETWORK (WN)

2.4GHZ AND 5.0GHZ

Most routers nowadays come with a 2.4 and 5.0GHz Wireless network configuration for both you and your Guest. Avoid sharing and mixing your devices with devices from your Guest.

We define a Guest who does not live with you or when you don't want them having access to your devices on your private network.

For example, I have all my computers on a separate router. All other computers, smartphones, and devices that my wife and kids use are on their router/network. This allows them to use printer and other resources within the same network.

In some cases, if you have kids causing issues within your network, we recommend getting them a separate router or bumping them to your Guest network.

Please make sure that you avoid using the **same** Wi-Fi name for both the 2.4 and 5.0GHz. You can use the same password, but not the same Wi-Fi name. Sometimes, ISP will configure your 2.4 and 5.0 with the same Wi-Fi name.

IOT DEVICES

We also recommend connecting any Internet of Things (IoT) devices to the Guest network. IoT include devices like Echo from Alexa or wall Plugs that you control from your Smartphone. All IoT should be configured on your Guest Network and not part of your private network.

If you have your own business or company computers, we highly recommend having another router strictly for your own network that keeps your personal network away from your business network.

DISABLE GUEST WI-FI.

If you are not going to use the guest Wi-Fi on your router, we recommend to still **protect** your guest Wi-Fi by replacing the default SSID and password with your own credentials.

Please log into your router to rename the Guest 2.4 and 5.0 Wi-Fi names to something different from your Wi-Fi names. Next, add a unique password/passphrase to both 2.4 and 5.0 Guest Wi-Fi as well. Once you have completed these two steps, then DISABLE your guest Wi-Fi, afterwards.

LIST OF IoT

Every IoT device comes with their own Mac Address. First, let us define what a Mac Address is (Wikipedia):

Tech version:

- A Media Access Control (MAC) address is a unique identifier assigned to a network interface controller for use as a network address in communications within a network segment. This use is common in most IEEE 802 networking technologies, including Ethernet, Wi-Fi, and Bluetooth.

Non-Tech Version:

- Think of a MAC address like your social security number. Every computer, smartphone, and device come with a unique MAC address. If you want to know what the MAC address is for each device, go into their settings.

When it comes to IoT devices, you will be surprised of the names that come with some of these IoT devices. Our recommendation is to change the name to something easy for you to distinguish them based on the location and who is using them.

Please document all IoT device information in your password secrets notebook. List the name, owner of the device, and MAC address for each IoT device.

Remember, to use your Guest Wi-Fi for all your IoT devices. Once again, all this is somewhat tekkie, please reach out and we will be happy to explain.

PASSWORD SECRETS NOTEBOOK SAMPLES

INTERNET SERVICE PROVIDER (ISP)

Name Account # Fees

Best Phone # Alternative

Date Promised Speeds (Mbps) →

Your IP Address VPN IP Address

ROUTER FACTORY DEFAULT SETTINGS

Model Serial #

Admin URL /IP Address Quarterly Firmware Updates

Login Username Router's PW

NEW ROUTER SETTINGS

Admin URL/IP Address Mac Address (Optional)

Login Username Router's PW

Recovery Questions or Email (optional)

WIRELESS NETWORK (WN) FOR 2.4 & 5.0 GHZ

Your SSID/WN names PW/Passphrase 2.4 5.0

I have turned on or enable my Guest Network ☐ Yes, enabled ☐ No, not enabled

Guest SSID or WN names PW/Passphrase 2.4 5.0

LIST OF COMPUTERS, PRINTERS*, PHONES, & DEVICES

#	Name of Device	Owner of Device/Location	Mac Address	IP Address (Optional)
1				
2				
3				
4				
5				
6				
7				
8				
9				
10				
11				
12				
13				
14				
15				
16				
17				
18				
19				
20				

* Always use a static IP address for printers versus having a dynamic IP Address

CHAPTER

7

OTHER PEOPLE & YOUR CREDIT CARD HISTORY

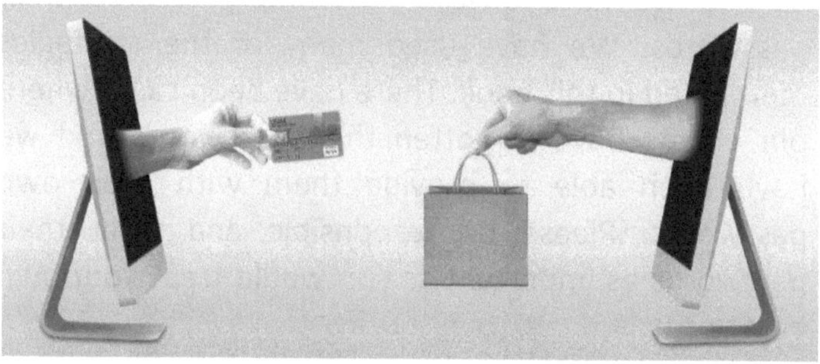

OTHER PEOPLE'S PASSWORDS

Many times, other people like your spouse, kids, family members (mostly your parents), friends, and other people might one day share a password with you because they trust you. When someone provides you with their passwords, please take it seriously and be fully responsible to protect their information.

Many of our clients have shared their passwords with us and we have always password protected their passwords. We have used many of the strategies mentioned in this book. There have been cases where our clients have forgotten their passwords and we have been able to provide them with their own passwords. Please be responsible and treat their passwords as important as you would treat your own passwords.

OTHER PEOPLE YOU SHARED PASSWORDS WITH

It is also especially important to also document in the password secrets notebook all the people you have shared your passwords with, especially the passwords that range from your thumb down to your ring finger. With the pinky passwords, you don't really have to worry too much about those.

YOUR KID'S PASSWORDS

Being a dad of three, I will say that when it comes to knowing your kid's passwords, please be polite and explain to your kids why you need their passwords. Avoid forcing them to give you their passwords. For one thing, they can easily change it on you, especially if they don't want to share the password with you in the first place. My wife and I have learned that you want to always **RESPECT** your kid's privacy, especially with teenagers. Instead of forcing to get their passwords, explain and educate them on the reasons why you will need to obtain their passwords.

HIRING FREELANCERS AND PROFESSIONALS

When hiring any type of freelancer or professional that requires you to give them your passwords, make sure to always <u>plan ahead by setting up and providing them with a temporary, but different password</u> from your main or original password.

Try to make this temporary password easy for them to remember and apply, because in some cases they will have to enter the password multiple times. Plus, you never want to give them any hints or ideas of the style of passwords you use.

With some accounts, you can make freelancers and professionals <u>managers or assistants</u> under that account. QuickBooks and WordPress, for example, allows you to add people with different roles which prevent them from noting your master password for the account, giving them limited access to your account while they do work for you.

For example, many of my clients have gone to their local cell phone carriers to set up their Apple or Google phones and most of the time the representative will ask to provide them with their main password.

Please don't provide them with your main password, especially if that password is used with other accounts. Instead, prepare ahead of time by changing your password temporarily and setup a password that you will never use in the future. Never give any freelancer and/or professional any of your passwords, especially passwords that range from your thumb to middle finger type of passwords.

YOUR CREDIT CARD HISTORY

With many of your accounts, companies tend to ask you to provide them with the last four digits of your credit card. To make it easier on yourself, and anyone who has access to your account, please document in the password secrets notebook the account name, credit type, the last four digits used, and when it is going to expire, because we can tell you from our own personal experience that when we close down or replace our credit cards, we don't have any idea what the last four digits of those old credit cards were.

PASSWORD SECRETS NOTEBOOK SAMPLES

OTHER people's password that you must **KEEP**	
Person's Name	
Account	
Username/ID	
Password	
Person's Name	
Account	
Username/ID	
Password	
Person's Name	
Account	
Username/ID	
Password	
Person's Name	
Account	
Username/ID	
Password	
Person's Name	
Account	
Username/ID	
Password	
Person's Name	
Account	
Username/ID	
Password	
Person's Name	
Account	
Username/ID	
Password	

OTHER people who I SHARED my password with

Person's Name

Account

Username/ID

Password you shared

Person's Name

Account

Username/ID

Password you shared

Person's Name

Account

Username/ID

Password you shared

Person's Name

Account

Username/ID

Password you shared

Person's Name

Account

Username/ID

Password you shared

Person's Name

Account

Username/ID

Password you shared

Person's Name

Account

Username/ID

Password you shared

KID'S PASSWORDS

#	Account/Social Media	Username	Password	Kid's name
1				
2				
3				
4				
5				
6				
7				
8				
9				
10				
11				
12				
13				
14				
15				
16				
17				
18				
19				
20				

HIRING FREELANCERS AND/OR PROFESSIONALS

Freelancer Name	Account	Username/ID	Password Given

Freelancer Name	Account	Username/ID	Password Given

Freelancer Name	Account	Username/ID	Password Given

Freelancer Name	Account	Username/ID	Password Given

Freelancer Name	Account	Username/ID	Password Given

CREDIT CARD HISTORY

Account Name Credit Card Type Last 4 Digits Expired On

Notes

Account Name Credit Card Type Last 4 Digits Expired On

Notes

Account Name Credit Card Type Last 4 Digits Expired On

Notes

Account Name Credit Card Type Last 4 Digits Expired On

Notes

Account Name Credit Card Type Last 4 Digits Expired On

Notes

Account Name Credit Card Type Last 4 Digits Expired On

Notes

Account Name Credit Card Type Last 4 Digits Expired On

Notes

ADDITIONAL NOTES SECTION

CHAPTER

8

RESOURCES

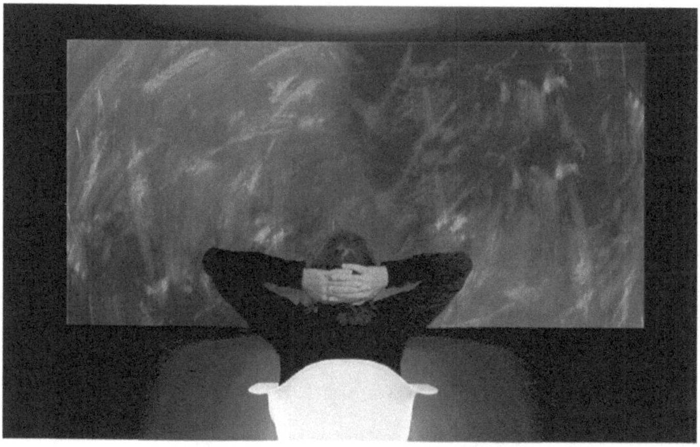

PASSWORD SECRETS NOTEBOOK PURCHASE

To purchase your very own Password Secrets Notebook, please visit the following website:

www.TekkieTeks.com/Products

For more support help or answer any questions regarding what is in this book or just need some support help, please visit us the following website:

www.TekkieTeks.com

OUR MEMBERSHIP BENEFITS

UNLIMITED EXPERT IT SUPPORT

We at TekkieTeks give you UNLIMITED monthly support for all your general tech questions, updates, and maintenance of your IT Assets. These IT Assets include Desktops and Laptops with either Mac or Windows operating systems.

MALWARE AND VIRUS PROTECTION

Peace of mind is what TekkieTeks strive for our clients. Since 1998, we have prevented well over 1 billion infections. We remotely connection to your computer to remove any Malware or Viruses that are causing poor performance and issues on your computer.

We will check your existing protection. If we feel you need to upgrade, we will recommend the Internet Security and VPN protection we have used with many of our clients.

ADDITION REMOTE SUPPORT MEMBERSHIP BENEFITS

Mac, PC, Phones, and Tablet Support	Software Uninstalls and Installs
Mac or PC Malware or Virus Removal	Password Reset
Diagnostic and Troubleshooting	Wire and Wireless Network Setup
Software Troubleshooting & Repair	Wire or Wireless Printer Setup
Computer Tune-up and Cleaning	Printer Troubleshooting
Local and Online Email Setup	All General Monthly Questions

EXTRAS, DISCOUNTS, & SUPPORT AS NEEDED

INTERNET SECURITY AND VPN PROTECTION

For an additional fee per year per device, TekkieTeks will include a license on either your PC or Mac computers with strong Internet Security and VPN protection.

On-Site Visits (AZ only)

You only pay an additional fee per ON-SITE visits where we can physically come to your place of business or residence to offer standard installations, services, and physically configure any of your IT Assets you purchased from us or from any other vendor.

10% OFF

You will get 10% off any additional special support outside of the monthly membership.

15% OFF

You will get 15% off every future courses and products your purchase from TekkieTeks.

SPECIAL AS NEEDED SUPPORT ON:

- Full Restoration of Computer
- Reclaimed Hacked Computers
- Basic Data Transfer & Data Backup
- Level 1 Data Recovery
- Data Transfer from PC to Mac
- Home or Business New Wi-Fi Setup
- Data Transfer from Mac to PC
- Microsoft Exchange Email Setup
- Data Transfer from PC to PC
- Data Files and Picture Organization
- Data Transfer from Mac to Mac
- Setting up your Smart Phones

THREE MEMBERSHIP PLANS

Monthly	Semi-Annually	Yearly
Crafted for New Clients	Crafted for semi experienced Clients	Crafted for clients who are not Tekkie
$40/month	$37/month	$33/month
A Month to Month fee that can be cancelled at anytime	Every other month contract for six months	12-month contract designed to save money and fewer headaches
These monthly fees will change with time, please visit **www.TekkieTeks.com** for the latest monthly fees and changes.		

FREE TEKKIE TUESDAYS WEBINAR

Supporting clients is our mission. We have our Free Bi-Weekly Tekkie Tuesdays Webinar.

Please join us on the 2nd and 4th Tuesday of every month for training and answering any technical questions. Our LIVE Q&A TekkieTuesdays Webinar will focus on subjects around:

- Mac or PC desktop/laptop/tablet and Printers or other Peripherals
- IT Support issues related to Mac, PC, & Mobile devices
- Tools on Protecting & Organizing your documents, pictures, & videos
- Preventing Viruses, Malware & Computer common issues
- Backing up data files on your PC, & Mobile devices
- Most important, how to Destroy, Donate, Refurbish, or Reuse your IT Assets

Please go to **www.TekkieTeks.com/TekkieTues** and "Subscribe" to be added to our Webinar invite. We always WELCOME you to invite or bring family members, friends, and other entrepreneurs.

URGENT IT SUPPORT

If you are experiencing urgent issues with your computers, smartphone, devices, and/or printers. Or simply just need help to understand the ever-changing hardware and software, please submit a ticket and our WeCare team at TekkieTeks will get back to you as quickly as possible. Please visit our website link at **www.TekkieTeks.com/Urgent** to get your ticket request started.

Thank you for reaching out to our WeCare team at TekkieTeks, and we will reach out to you as fast we can. Please provide us with your contact information, best time to call, and a brief description of your issue or urgency. Thank you in advance.

ABOUT THE AUTHOR

Lorenzo Zesati is the founder and CEO of TekkieTeks, a company who takes pride in working and supporting Creators and Entrepreneurs with IT and Business Growth needs.

Lorenzo graduated with an engineering degree from California State University of Long Beach (CSULB) and served two terms as President for the Society of Hispanic Professional Engineers (SHPE). Lorenzo continued his education with University of California at Santa Barbara (UCSB) as a Research Engineer and he is graduate Member from the Dale Carnegie Training.

Lorenzo became the Director of Leads Club for three straight years. Leads Club gives business owners and entrepreneurs a way to expand their business in a professional environment that gets results. Lorenzo was an active board member for the Inventor's Association of Arizona (IAA).

Lorenzo has been coaching and training creators and entrepreneurs understand the various business and technology barriers involved in learning to implement solutions in their endeavors. Lorenzo loves baseball and continues to coach young kids and has

volunteering coaching at the Young Men's Christian Association (YMCA).
Lorenzo loves talking and speaking about his books, entrepreneurship, and inventions. As a keynote speaker and with his amazing personal and professional experiences, he can empower organizations, schools, and communities.

Lorenzo is an Author, Baseball Coach, Business Engineer, IT Support Specialist, Inventor, and Speaker. Lorenzo continues to create and deliver products and solutions to his clients to bring their company and ideas to market. His mind never stops and his enthusiasm and passion for helping businesses move forward is extraordinary.

Lorenzo's Mission:

Transform Entrepreneurs Into Creators and

Transform Creators into Entrepreneurs

To impact the world through STEAM awareness, support, and development

Lorenzo lives in Arizona with his amazing wife Michelle who have been married since 2000. Between the two them, they have two girls and one boy.

Made in United States
Troutdale, OR
11/03/2026

56845097R00096